# Culture, Context & Content

## A Short Guide to Interpreting Your Bible

## David F Mansfield

ISBN: 978-1-4452-4374-0

the haven

A ministry of The Haven Church
www.havenchurch.org.uk

# Contents

# Acknowledgements

It would not be right to put something into print without acknowledging the wonderful input, teaching, training, mentoring and encouragement I have received over the years.

The following is a short and by no means exhaustive list of those who did something that made a difference in my life through taking the time to give me some instruction!

My love and gratitude goes out to;

The Rt Revd Christopher Morgan, Bishop of Colchester

Barry Manson

Dr David Petts

Dr Andrew Davies

Dr John Andrews

John Pettifor


And, of course, my beautiful wife, Sue, without whom I would be much thinner! Love as always Babe!

And my three inspiring daughters, your faith, commitment and passion to serve God are a constant challenge to me.

# Who is this book for?

This is a book for everyone. We all need to understand the basics on Bible interpretation if we are to make proper sense of it.

It is by no means exhaustive and there are many excellent books to be found that will take this subject much further – there is a list of suggestions at the end of this book. I offer this as a simple guide to help those who want to go deeper and be sure that their conclusions on the Biblical text are well founded.

For the serious Bible student, this should serve as a concise reminder and encouragement towards due diligence when studying.

For the more casual reader, it should serve as a tool to ensure a better interpretation as we pursue a greater understanding of our God.

Whatever level of study you engage in, I trust you will find something of use that will help you to engage more fully with the Word of God, discover his perfect will and have it impact the whole of your life.

# Introduction

## Anecdotal versus systematic study

Much of what we receive today from our teachers and preachers is anecdotal. That is to say reflections of personal experiences which are then given a [usually quite loose] Biblical context. Although this is not wrong, the main problem with this method is that the Biblical "context" is not always accurate or appropriate!

For instance, we pray for someone to be healed, God heals them, we then tell the story adding some scriptures about healing and teach that, if we follow the model, everyone will get healed. It is easily done and, whether the final point is true or not, our journey to reach it is flawed.

When we are making decisions about theology, doctrine and the essentials of our faith and practice, it is vitally important that we do not build our arguments on anecdotes and scriptures that seem to fit.

The Apostle Paul says that prophecy should be weighed[1], but how do you weigh it? We are taught to make ourselves accountable to one another, but how will we define what we are accountable for?[2] We are told to guard our doctrine. What exactly are we guarding?[3]

---

1 1Corinthians 14:29.

2 Hebrews 13:17

3 Titus 1,9

False doctrines are constantly trying to worm their way into the church, how do we measure what is right and wrong?[4]

This is where proper Bible study comes into its own. Proper systematic study helps us to understand all of the important things; who God is, what he thinks about stuff, what pleases him, what makes him angry, etc. This will give us something to weigh the rest against.

**A word about doctrine**

Doctrine is the name we give to the beliefs that we think are important and foundational to our faith. Doctrine, again, is established through proper study and interpretation. We wouldn't want to base our beliefs on things that God did not say or did not mean! If we get our doctrine right then we really do have something solid to measure everything else against.

# The need for proper interpretation

A Sunday school teacher was discussing the Ten Commandments with her five and six year-olds.

After explaining the commandment to "honour" your Father and your Mother, she asked, "Is there a commandment that teaches us how to treat our brothers and sisters?"

Without missing a beat, one little boy (the oldest of a family) answered, "You shall not kill."

---

4 2Timothy 4:3

Well, that's one interpretation!

I well remember in my Bible College days, the Principal coming in to class to gives us a lecture fresh from the class next door. He didn't look happy. One of his earlier students had suggested that we take the Bible on "face value". In a College renowned for its academic values and its exegetical excellence, this was nothing short of sacrilege.

The whole point of being there was to learn to correctly interpret the Scriptures so that we can discern an appropriate application.

If we don't pay careful attention to our interpretation, then we might end up with a church where women must wear hats and never speak, and men will be forming a queue at the barber's. We would be stuck with a life where God is only with us if there are two or three of us gathered together, whilst believing that we are superhuman and can do absolutely anything we want if we would only have faith!

Clearly, "face value" will get us in to trouble.

The purpose of this book is to give you some basic tools to help in the process of understanding God's message to us in the Bible.

# Where do we begin?

I want to suggest we start with three basic processes, or questions to ask which will help us to make better sense of our Bible. These questions cover three specific areas;

- Culture
- Context
- Content

## Culture

Culture can be defined as;

*"The attitudes and behaviour characteristics of a particular social group."*

When we look at culture we are looking at a certain place, in a certain time, containing a certain people. Understanding culture will help build a background image to set the rest of our interpretation against.

## Context

This may be defined as;

*"The circumstances that form the setting for an event, statement, or idea, and in terms of which it can be fully understood and assessed"*

Context asks the "who, what, why, where, when and how" questions that give us the immediate picture of what is going on.

## Content

This simply refers to;

*"The things that are held or included in the passage"*

Having taken the two previous steps, we can then examine the content and discover its meaning and application.

So now let's begin to grapple with these processes and see what we can discover about the right way to interpret our Bible.

# Culture

*"The attitudes and behaviour characteristics of a particular social group."*

Understanding culture requires an investigation into the time, the place and the people. It's about understanding the historical, social and cultural background to the passage.

## Time

Placing scripture into its historical setting [the time] is vitally important.

To truly understand the world Jesus was born into requires at least a basic understanding of Jewish, Roman and Greek history. Our study should help us to understand the political situation, the economic situation and the religious atmosphere surrounding events.

## Place

We need to understand the traditions and customs of the setting that the text is placed in, the surrounding political and religious practices, and how they affect people. An example of this would be the fact that Israel was a country under occupation. The geographical location and all that it involves. All of these things make a big difference to our reading of the text.

For example, if you have never visited a hot, dry and dusty country that struggles to find water, you can never really get the full effect of...

*John 7,37 On the last and greatest day of the Feast, Jesus stood and said in a loud voice, "If anyone is thirsty, let him come to me and drink. 38 Whoever believes in me, as the Scripture has said, streams of living water will flow from within him."*

## People

People's lives were very different in Bible times, so their perceptions of life will have been very different. They will not have had the same attitudes towards, or expectations of, life that we will have. They did not have the benefit of modern science [although some might consider that a handicap!] or experience of the sort of religious and political freedoms we have today. In short, their thinking would have been different. The more we understand about their culture, the more we will understand about their mindset.

## Understanding the background to a passage

The following passage in Luke is a useful example of this principle;

*Luke 10:38 As Jesus and his disciples were on their way, he came to a village where a woman named Martha opened her home to him. 39 She had a sister called Mary, who sat at the Lord's feet listening to what he said. 40 But Martha was distracted by all the preparations that had to be made. She came to him and asked, "Lord, don't you care that my sister has left me to do the work by myself? Tell her to help me!"*

*41 "Martha, Martha," the Lord answered, "you are worried and upset about many things, 42 but only one thing is needed. Mary has chosen what is better, and it will not be taken away from her."*

Cultural issues we should consider when reading this passage; hospitality, social settings, and the place of women.

Women were kept separate from men, they had their own spaces in any communal gathering. Women would sit separate from the men, their place was literally in the kitchen or the bedroom.

Rabbis would not normally accept women disciples. It goes against the cultural norm for Mary to sit at the feet of Jesus listening to him teach.

Martha knew this and expected her sister to be sent back to the kitchen immediately!

Understanding this about the culture helps us see that there is something much more than "my sister has left me to do the work by myself" going on. Jesus, placating Martha, allows and endorses Mary's occupation of a position normally reserved for a man. What is He saying in "Mary has chosen what is better" ?

Clearly, in its cultural setting, Mary has chosen to be a man! She is breaking out of the cultural norms and kicking against the pressure placed on her by society to follow Jesus. Jesus, the great liberator, endorses her decision and encourages her by pronouncing that, even though it kicks against their norms, she has chosen the best thing. She has chosen not to be bound by man-made rules and culture and to follow Jesus. Not only that, but she is not to return to her subjugated state.

This action must have had a serious impact on the other guests. This is not simply an account of a woman choosing worship over work, although this on its own would have caused enough offence. This is a woman taking a man's position to follow Jesus, breaking out of the culture. An endorsement from Jesus must have created quite a stir, elevating Mary from her traditional status to that of a man. This is a clear signal that women occupy a place of equal value with men in the Kingdom of God.

Without the background information you could be forgiven for thinking it's all about "spending time with friends is more important than cooking the dinner" as I once heard someone preach! This passage is one of the great liberation passages that shows Jesus' respect for women and His common practice of elevating them above the surrounding circumstances.

Without doing our cultural homework, we would miss the principal impact of this text.

# Context

*"The circumstances that form the setting for an event, statement, or idea, and in terms of which it can be fully understood and assessed"*

Context is all about asking important questions about what is going on. It's the who, why, what, where sort of questions that help us to see what is going on.

The following passage from Philippians will show us the importance of understanding the context;

*Phil. 4:10-13 I rejoice greatly in the Lord that at last you have renewed your concern for me. Indeed, you have been concerned, but you had no opportunity to show it. 11 I am not saying this because I am in need, for I have learned to be content whatever the circumstances. 12 I know what it is to be in need, and I know what it is to have plenty. I have learned the secret of being content in any and every situation, whether well fed or hungry, whether living in plenty or in want. 13 I can do everything through him who gives me strength.*

Areas that are important to consider; Can I really do "everything" [anything?] because of Jesus?

Verse 13 can be found printed, in isolation, on pictures, wrist bands, mugs, tee shirts etc. Many people take this to mean that we should be supermen [or super women] and condemn themselves as lacking in faith when they find that they can't.

So, let's ask some context questions about this passage;

What is the immediate background to this comment?

Paul is talking to the Philippians about his struggles in ministry, partly due to the lack of support from them. His point is that, even without their help, God has given him strength and he is achieving his objectives.

If he can do anything at all, why has he not just taken himself out of this situation? Clearly that is not an option – if it was then any sane person would take it.

Understanding the immediate context helps us to understand that we can't just choose something we like and God will give us strength to do it. In its context, Paul is saying that God has given him strength to continue in, and be successful in, the ministry that God has called him to.

Understanding this in context keeps us from the naivety of expecting that we can do anything. I'm sure that, if this were true, some of us would have won the world for Jesus many years ago!

What the context does give us is a genuine confidence that God will strengthen us to do all that He has called us to, in good times and in bad and, ultimately, grant us success.

Therefore, "I can do everything [I have been called to do – in this specific case 'endure being in need'] through him who gives me strength" is a much better understanding of the text.

Sometimes we need to read wider than just a few verses either side to get a better view of the context. In the

Gospels we want to see where it all fits in the context of Jesus' journey for instance.

Luke 15 is another good example. We find "the prodigal son" in this chapter, but if we take a closer look at the context, we see the chapter starts with the Pharisees as part of the audience, and they are complaining about Jesus spending time with sinners. Observing this context would lead us to rename the parable "the angry brother", as this appears to be His primary point!

As we examine the context, we must also pay attention to the writing style of the text.

## Understanding genre

The Biblical method of study takes particular attention to genre. It recognises that there are different types of literature and treats them accordingly. This is an important step in establishing context.

There are nine generally recognised styles of writing; narrative, prophecy, wisdom, psalm, poetry, gospel, parable, epistle and apocalyptic.

Understanding the style will tell us which filter to process the text through. **Narrative** writing is usually giving us a chronological, historical account normally written [but not exclusively] by eye witnesses. The fact that it's history doesn't stop it being theology, but knowing that it's history helps us to interpret it properly.

The **Prophetic** style has God speaking directly to us through His chosen mouth piece. Through the Prophet, He imparts instruction, wisdom and vision for the future.

**Poetry** paints pictures with words. The writers draw us into understanding through earthly images that present heavenly concepts. Much Hebrew poetry uses a technique called **parallelism**, this is a form of repetition the can reinforce or develop the point.

For instance;

*Job 5,10 He bestows rain on the earth; he sends water upon the countryside. 11 The lowly he sets on high, and those who mourn are lifted to safety. 12 He thwarts the plans of the crafty, so that their hands achieve no success. 13 He catches the wise in their craftiness, and the schemes of the wily are swept away. 14 Darkness comes upon them in the daytime; at noon they grope as in the night. 15 He saves the needy from the sword in their mouth; he saves them from the clutches of the powerful. 16 So the poor have hope, and injustice shuts its mouth.*

This whole passage uses parallelism, and verse 14 is a particularly good example.

**Psalms** are quite literally songs. Some to be performed, some for corporate worship, some for the journey.

The **Gospels** are narratives that tell the story of the incarnate Jesus. They record His teaching, His actions, His journey and His sacrifice. The Gospels include **parables** which are short fictional stories designed to make a point.

It is worth mentioning at this point that most teaching in the Bible is metaphorical. That is to say that it takes common earthly imagery to describe heavenly principles which, otherwise, might be impossible for us to understand. For instance, Jesus' many references to agriculture or Paul calling the church "a body", are clear earthly images that we can relate to, and help us to grasp eternal concepts.

The **Epistles** are literally letters written to the early church or to individuals within it. They contain teaching and encouragement, and occasional insights into New Testament culture. Most of our doctrine is drawn from these letters.

The **Wisdom** writings contain sound bites that give us wise patterns for living.

And finally, **Apocalyptic** writings contain images of hope in times of trouble for God's people. Often futuristic, they are designed, in the face of a corrupt world, to help us focus on the God who will help us to stand. This type of writing can be quite complicated and requires much diligence in interpreting. Revelation, the last book in the Bible, is a good illustration of apocalyptic writing.

# Content

*"The things that are held or included in the passage"*

This involves determining what actual point is.

*Acts 1,8 But you will receive power when the Holy Spirit comes on you; and you will be my witnesses in Jerusalem, and in all Judea and Samaria, and to the ends of the earth."*

Areas to consider; If I am a member of a local church, what are the parameters of my ministry?

A closer inspection of this text [examining the words], reveals the global responsibility of all believers.

Many have taught along the lines of "Jerusalem is mine, you go to Judea". This thinking is clearly not Biblical. The command is for **all of God's people** to take responsibility for **all of the world**.

How we do that is perhaps a bigger question, but the command is clear. We [His disciples] have a responsibility for where we are and the rest of the world stretching out from there. Overseas mission doesn't necessarily, for most of us, mean going for your whole life, but short term missions would seem to be an adequate fulfilment of the command. However we express it, whether it be crossing the world or crossing the street, we have a global responsibility.

The passage informs me then, to wait until the Spirit has come, then directs me to be a witness.

Some might want to say that this passage only relates to the original hearers and excludes us. This is grounds for gaining a better understanding of the context.

In the wider context of the Gospels, Jesus' strategy is to teach the disciples the things they need to teach others in order for the mission to be accomplished.

*Matt. 28,18 Then Jesus came to them and said, "All authority in heaven and on earth has been given to me. [19] Therefore go and make disciples of all nations, baptizing them in the name of the Father and of the Son and of the Holy Spirit, [20] and* **teaching them to obey everything I have commanded you.** *And surely I am with you always, to the very end of the age."*

It is not reasonable, or sustainable, to think that Jesus changed His mind on this at the last moment, therefore, the command is for all disciples.

If I have received the power, what am I waiting for?

## Asking the important questions

So, a proper examination of the content should give a clear practical application.

When examining the content, we should ask;

- Who is speaking?

- Who are they speaking to?

- What are they saying?

- What does that mean for us?

The last question here is the application question. If Jesus is speaking to us through His word, we need to understand, if we are to be obedient, what is required of us. We also don't want to saddle ourselves with something Jesus doesn't actually want us to do!

There are other tools we can use to examine the content...

## A handful of "Ologies"

When we are entering into a serious study of scripture, there a certain themes which we want to pick out of each author's writings. These themes build our theological base; they give us the blocks to build on when we think about personal discipleship, church and our mission. They come in the shape of six "ologies"!

Words that end in –ology usually mean the study of something. For example, the Greek word for God is theos so theology means the study of God.

### Christology

You might have already guessed that this has to do with the study of the Christ; Jesus! We want to observe, both through the clear statements and through the language used, what the writer believes about Jesus. This is important because, for instance, if you don't believe that Jesus is Lord why would you want to obey Him?

John's Gospel and Hebrews have a high Christology, they make great efforts to help us see who Jesus is; the glorious Son of the Living God. Both writers have Him eternal, fully God, fully human, the perfect sacrifice.

You might want to suggest that the whole of the Bible is about Jesus, and you would be right! But, clearly some writers have more to say about His person and work.

It is always good to ask the question "What does this teach me about Jesus?" Or, as Darrin Patrick would ask, "How is Jesus the Hero?"[5]

Asking questions of a text about Christology will help us to grow in our understanding of who our Saviour is.

**Pneumatology**

Pneuma is the Greek word for wind or spirit, so this means the study of the Holy Spirit.

Here we want to observe the way the Holy Spirit works and what we can expect from Him. If you don't believe that the Holy Spirit can heal people then why would you pray for the sick? Observing the person and work of the Spirit should encourage us to engage more with Him, allow Him to work more deeply in our lives and use us to the glory of God.

In the same way that we ask Christological questions, we should ask Pneumatological questions.

We should observe the wider work of the Spirit in circumstances and creation, and the personal work of

---

5 http://www.acts29network.org/acts-29-blog/preaching-the-mission-exegesis--application/

the Spirit in regeneration, guidance, empowerment and in being a "replacement Jesus".

It is always good to ask the question "How is the Holy Spirit working here?" The answer should help us to understand more about how the Holy Spirit wants to work in our lives.

## Soteriology

This means the study of salvation. How are we saved? Who does what? Is our salvation secure? If we don't understand the process of salvation then how do we know if we are saved? Has everything been done that needs to be done or is there something else we should be doing?

Soteriology helps give us confidence in our salvation.

## Eschatology

Eschatology is the study of the final stages of history. When will Jesus come back? What happens then? This helps us to know what to expect and to learn to read the seasons.

It includes a lot of Old Testament writings as they point to the climax of history.

This is a particularly difficult area as there are many different views on Eschatology, and many of them are Biblically sustainable.

The most helpful questions to ask of the text in this category would centre on the personal challenges of living expectant of the return of the Christ in His glory. This will serve to help us shape our lives in a God pleasing way and not be tempted by the lures of this word.

I read recently of a church that had decided to live like Jesus was coming back at the end of the month. Everybody's lives were dramatically changed. This is Eschatology at its best.

It is always good to ask the question "What does this have to say about the future and the way I am living my life?"

## Ecclesiology

This is the study of the church and how it is supposed to work. So, it looks at church government and leadership, church meetings, organisational structures, fellowship and community. This helps to give us a picture of what our life together is supposed to look like.

It should serve to guide us in leadership and pastoring, helping us to do things in an orderly and godly manner, and in a way that will cause the church to grow.

It also teaches us about accountability and community, two areas of life today that need special attention.

It is always good to ask the question "What is this text saying about how we do church?"

## Missiology

This is the study of the method and practice of mission. We have been given a commandment to reach the world.

How do we do it? Who should do it? Where should we do it? If we don't understand the mission we are going to have trouble fulfilling it.

Missiology shapes our thinking about how we do the works of Jesus in our local communities and around the world.

It is always good to ask the question "What does this teach me about reaching out to my neighbour?"

Whilst we will not find all of these "ologies" in every verse, it is surprising how many do turn up in just a few verses...

## Making it work...

Let's take the first few verses of Galatians and see how these "ologies" appear...

*Gal. 1,1 Paul, an apostle — sent not from men nor by man, but by Jesus Christ and God the Father, who raised him from the dead — 2 and all the brothers with me,*

*To the churches in Galatia:*

*Gal. 1,3 Grace and peace to you from God our Father and the Lord Jesus Christ, 4 who gave himself for our sins to rescue us from the present evil age, according to the will of our God and Father, 5 to whom be glory for ever and ever. Amen.*

We start with **ecclesiology**, Paul claims to be an apostle sent by God. The word apostle, in fact, means "sent one". Paul here flags up for us that there are offices in the church; appointments sanctioned by God, of which apostle is one, and he is an Apostle.

So, when we read about Paul's life and work, we are getting a glimpse of what it means to be an apostle. This helps us with our ecclesiology.

Also, "and all the brothers with me" gives us a glimpse of the early church community.

Paul is sent! Here we get some **missiology**, God sends people to accomplish His mission. Paul is sent by God to do the work of God.

Then we get some **christology**; Jesus Christ. He is acknowledging Jesus as the Christ, the promised deliverer.

In the same sentence we get some **soteriology**; raised from the dead, the centre of the Gospel – and we're not even out of the first verse yet!

In verses 3 & 4, we get some repeats. "Jesus Christ" is prefixed with "the Lord", leaving no doubt what Paul's view of Jesus is (christology). Then "who gave himself for our sins to rescue us..." continues with Paul's statements about salvation (soteriology).

Also, in verse 4 we get some **eschatology**; the present evil age. This is the part of history that we are now living in, the prelude to the second coming of Christ.

So you can see that as we work through this letter, by a mixture of terms used (the Lord) and clear statements (gave Himself for our sins), our theology grows, our understanding of the Bible deepens, and our lives are impacted by the revelation of truth which helps us to live out our calling.

At least, that's how it's supposed to work!

# Two common approaches to interpretation

## The Biblical approach

The Biblical approach to reading and interpreting the Bible focuses on treating each book in its own right.

So, when we read Matthew's Gospel, we read it like it's the only book we have. Treating it this way helps us to draw out every bit out of it that we can.

### The benefits of a Biblical approach

Maintaining a focus on one writer and his style, his purpose in writing and his intended audience will help us to gather more from the message.

We can get inside the head of the writer and experience more of what he is seeing and doing.

We are not distracted by what other writers think so we can fully process the views right in front of us.

### The pit-falls of a Biblical approach

Of course, there is always a danger of missing the point when we read a book in isolation. In John we read;

*John 20,21 Again Jesus said, "Peace be with you! As the Father has sent me, I am sending you." 22 And with that he breathed on them and said, "Receive the Holy Spirit.*

Some commentators interpret this as "John's Pentecost", the time when the Holy Spirit is poured out. Reading in isolation, you probably wouldn't want to question this. If you then read Luke's account in Acts 2, it is about as different as you can get and all the questions begin to emerge.

Both the texts are narrative, so style doesn't help us. A wider view is necessary, and a deeper analysis of both texts is called for.

When employing the Biblical approach, we still need to maintain a backdrop which includes the rest of the Bible in order that we work faithfully with all of the information available before taking a view.

## The Systematic Approach

Systematic;

*"done or acting according to a fixed plan or system; methodical"*

The systematic approach focuses more on themes and looks for those themes wherever they may be. A systematic approach draws together all the texts that deal with a specific subject and finds then the consistent view that is presented.

### The benefits of a systematic approach

A systematic approach involves comparing the text with other like texts. This approach is often used with the Gospels. Comparing context and content should confirm the right interpretation of the passage.

The same method can be used, for instance, with Paul's letters. Comparing similar passages should show some consistency of thought that will help us find the proper application.

## The pit-falls of a systematic approach

One of the problems that we face is in imagery. For instance, in Acts 2, tongues of fire are seen as the Holy Spirit baptising the believers. In other places, fire is seen as a sign of judgement. So we cannot just assume that fire means the same thing throughout. This is where a closer examination of context and content will help us.

## Making it work

A helpful issue to use would be one referred to earlier.

*Phil. 4,13 I can do everything through him who gives me strength.*

Using the systematic approach we can find passages that will support our established view that this is in context of the things that God calls us to do. For instance;

*1John 5,14 This is the confidence we have in approaching God: that if we ask anything according to his will, he hears us.*

John affirms that we can have confidence in God's help and He will hear us; if we ask according to His will.

Jesus makes the same point from a different angle;

*Matt. 6,31 So do not worry, saying, 'What shall we eat?' or 'What shall we drink?' or 'What shall we wear?' 32 For the pagans run after all these things, and your heavenly Father knows that you need them. 33 But seek first his kingdom and his righteousness, and all these things will be given to you as well.*

The systematic method gives a clear view that God's enabling and provision comes within the parameters of His will for the individual. If God has called me to walk on water He will empower me to do it. If He has not, why do I even want to try? But if I do try, I shouldn't rely on God's help if He hasn't called me to do it.

# An exercise

This passage from 1 Corinthians 13 has often been used as a proof text to say that the gifts of the Spirit ceased with establishment of the Canon of Scripture or the "end of the Apostolic age" [meaning the original Apostles have all died].

*1Cor. 13,8 Love never fails. But where there are prophecies, they will cease; where there are tongues, they will be stilled; where there is knowledge, it will pass away. 9 For we know in part and we prophesy in part, 10 but when perfection comes, the imperfect disappears. 11 When I was a child, I talked like a child, I thought like a child, I reasoned like a child. When I became a man, I put childish ways behind me. 12 Now we see but a poor reflection as in a mirror; then we shall see face to face. Now I know in part; then I shall know fully, even as I am fully known.*

The argument goes like this...

- The gifts will clearly at some point cease [8]

- They are imperfect anyway [9]

- When perfection comes [the completion of the scriptures, which we know as the Bible] these will pass away [10]

- The immaturity of the early church will give way to greater understanding and maturity [11]

- The poor reflection is brought into focus through the scriptures [12]

A proper exegesis of the passage, however, will produce a different view.

## Culture

- A review of the culture in which this passage is set reveals;

    - Difficult circumstances where a church has been built with people from a pluralistic Pagan background.

    - The influence of the local culture would give rise to a view of spirituality being defined by giftedness; "If you don't manifest a clearly supernatural gift then how can you be spiritual?"

## Context

- The immediate context of the passage has Paul giving remedial teaching into a tense situation where more than one voice is being heard by the people;

    - There are men trying usurp Paul's authority and preach a different message.

    - There is a spirit of competition/rivalry amongst the people, boasting about who prays in tongues the most etc.

    - The maturity that we think we have is flawed, we need to try to gain a better perspective.

- Placed between chapter 12 [a list of the gifts and a plea not to put them into a league table] and chapter 14 [defining the use of prophecy and tongues and encouraging the use of gifts that build up the church] it makes no sense for Paul to be saying "when we Apostles have finished our letters you won't need these anymore!" It defeats the object of writing the other two chapters.

  - Also, if this is what Paul meant, then he runs the risk of the Corinthians stopping using the gifts and claiming further perfection.

## Content

So what is Paul [clearly] saying?

- Paul's intention here is clearly to bring truth and balance in to place.
  - Love should cover all things. This is not a competition.
    - The gifts, that are being used as a symbol of status, are imperfect because of the imperfect vessels that are using them.
  - The gifts of the Spirit are temporary in nature and will, at some point, cease.

- This is important because it goes some way to removing the idea that they are a sign of status.

- If the gifts are to cease, we then should be more concerned with the giver than the gifts.

  - Clearly, in its immediate context, Paul expects the continuation of the gifts.

- The gifts will cease when perfection comes

  - When perfection comes I shall "see face to face" and "know fully"

  - Do I know fully when I read my Bible, or am I still in need of revelation?

  - Am I seeing Jesus face to face? Or is there more to come?

*"Nevertheless, it is difficult to prove the cessation of these gifts at the end of the first century A.D. by taking teleion [perfection] to refer to a completion of the canon at that time, since that idea is completely extraneous to the context. While teleion can and does refer to something completed at some time in the future, the time of that future completion is not suggested in v. 10 as being close.*

*On the other hand, in a number of contexts the related words telos ("end," "termination;" "last part") and teleo ("bring to an end") are used in relation to the second coming of Christ. This is true in both non-Pauline writing (cf. James 5:11; Rev 20:5, 7; 21:6; 22:13) and 1 Corinthians 1:8; 15:24. Since in the contexts of the Second Coming these related words are used and since Paul himself used telos in talking about the Second*

*Coming elsewhere in 1 Corinthians, it seems more normal to understand teleion in v.10 to mean that "perfection" is to come about at the Second Coming, or, if before, when the Christian dies and is taken to be with the Lord (2Cor 5:1-10)."[6]*

*"**8-13** The future of love is guaranteed. **9** In this transient existence our imperfect knowledge is reflected in our prophecy. **10** When perfection comes in heaven, then the imperfect will fall away. **12** Imperfect reflections will be replaced by true perception—imperfect mirrors distorted a proper reflection of the face in the mirror. Partial knowledge will give way to full knowledge, just as we are fully known by God. **13** Permanence is only given to faith, hope—the future comes to us from the hands of a God who will not fail us—and love. Love has the top place, for reasons that are clear in vs 1-7."[7]*

- If I am not yet perfected [which I don't expect to happen before Jesus returns and perfects me] then, by clear implication, the gifts will still be of considerable use to me.

So, properly interpreted, this passage is a plea for balance, for love, and for the removal of competition and the quest for status. It is designed to promote the right use of the gifts until the second coming of Christ, at which point, having been perfected, we will no longer need the gifts.

---

[6] The Expositor's Bible Commentary, Frank E. Gaebelein, Ed., Zondervan Publishing House.

[7] New Bible Commentary, University and Colleges Christian Fellowship

This exercise shows the need for proper exegesis in order to form a right view of the meaning of scripture and the theology we form from it.

This book has really only scratched the surface of this subject. If you are serious about your Biblical studies, there are many good books that develop this theme further. If you are a Pastor or Teacher, then developing this area is vital. Invest in yourself!

## Further reading on this subject...

**New Testament Exegesis**: A Handbook for Students and Pastors by Gordon D. Fee

**Elements of Biblical Exegesis**: A Basic Guide for Students and Ministers by Michael J. Gorman

**Biblical Exegesis**: A Beginner's Handbook by John H. Hayes and Carl R. Holladay

**How to Read the Bible for All Its Worth** by Gordon D. Fee and Douglas Stuart

**IVP Introduction to the Bible**: Story, Themes and Interpretation by Philip Johnston

# Book recommendations

Books are important. We need them to aid our study, to learn from people who are smarter than we are! My own little library is split between development books and reference books. Development books are the sort of books you read from cover to cover for your own personal growth. Reference books are books that we dip into to find relevant information on the topic we are studying.

The following are reference books I use regularly in my own studies, I trust these will help you in your own development.

## Bibles

**Today's New International Version**, Hodder & Stoughton

**English Standard Version**, Good News Publishers

**The Message**, Navpress [remember that this is a paraphrase and not strictly a translation]

I have 18 different translations in my Bible Software package, the above are the ones I use the most.

## Interlinear

An interlinear places the english translation underneath the Greek/Hebrew so you can get a better idea of the original text. For those of us who don't excel at languages, this is a really useful tool.

**The Interlinear NIV Parallel New Testament in Greek and English**, Zondervan

**The Interlinear NIV Hebrew-English Old Testament**, Zondervan

## Commentaries/Study Bibles

These will provide you with some scholarly observations on the text, and often some useful background information to aid your understanding.

**The Expositor's Bible Commentary**, Zondervan

**English Standard Version (ESV) Study Bible**, Good News Publishers.

**New Bible Commentary**, University and Colleges Christian Fellowship

**Zondervan NIV Bible Commentary**, Zondervan

**An introduction to the New Testament** by D. A. Carson and Douglas J. Moo

**An Introduction to the Old Testament** by Tremper Longman III & Raymond B. Dillard

## CDROM

These days I do most of study on my laptop. It's much more efficient and gives me my most used books at my fingertips!  Not all of the books I use have been digitised yet, so I still have to leaf through pages occasionally, but if you want a good starting point for a digital library, here's a good place to start;

**The Essential IVP Reference Collection**: The Complete Electronic Bible Study Resource (CD-ROM)

This CDROM is available from Amazon and contains the following books;

- Dictionary of Biblical Imagery
- Dictionary of Jesus and the Gospels
- Dictionary of New Testament Background
- Dictionary of Paul and His Letters
- Dictionary of the Later New Testament & Its Developments
- Hard Sayings of the Bible
- IVP Bible Background Commentary: New Testament
- IVP Bible Background Commentary: Old Testament
- IVP-Pocket Dictionaries:

- Study of NT Greek
- Biblical Studies
- Apologetics & Philosophy of Religion
- King James Version Bible
- New Bible Atlas
- New Bible Commentary
- New Bible Dictionary
- New Dictionary of Biblical Theology
- New Dictionary of Theology

You can add books to this software and it is available for Mac and PC. I currently have over 50 books and Bibles on mine, and there are more becoming available regularly.

## Internet

The following sites contain a number of useful resources;

http://www.biblegateway.com

http://www.biblestudytools.com/

http://www.christnotes.org/

http://www.studylight.org/com/

http://biblos.com/

http://www.easyenglish.info/bible-commentary/index.htm

http://www.searchgodsword.org/com/

http://net.bible.org/home.php

http://unbound.biola.edu/

That should be enough to get you going!